HEAR THE COLOUR

JOE NEAL

Copyright © 2015 Joe Neal

All rights reserved. No part of this publication may be reproduced or transmitted in any form or by any means, electronic or mechanical including photocopying, recording or any information storage or retrieval system, without prior permission in writing from the publishers.

The right of Joe Neal to be identified as the author of this work has been asserted by him in accordance with the Copyright, Designs and Patents Act 1988.

First published in the United Kingdom in 2015 by
The Choir Press

ISBN 978-1-910864-13-5

Printed in 11pt Cambria
Edited by Harriet Evans
Portrait of the author by Tommy Clancy
Cover illustration: Garden Tiger Moth

ALSO BY JOE NEAL

Telling It at a Slant, Pen Press (2013).
ISBN 978 1 78003 664 9

Turn Now the Tide, Choir Press (2014).
ISBN 978 1 909300 73 6

Readings by the author from these poetry collections can be heard at:

www.joenealtellingitataslant.com
www.turnnowthetide.com
www.hearthecolour.com

ABOUT THE AUTHOR

Joe Neal was born half-way up a mountain in North Wales. He began his acting career in repertory theatre before attending Nottingham University. To supplement his income, he also trained as a journalist, working for the Western Mail (Cardiff), Times, Guardian, Daily Telegraph and Daily Express.

As an actor, he has performed on stage, radio and television in Britain and Ireland. Between acting work Neal writes extensively on the countryside and natural history as well as devoting time to poetry and short stories which he believes should be read aloud – 'even to oneself.'

A glutton for punishing experiences, he stood twice as an Independent for Parliament in Britain and once in Ireland for the European elections.

His published work has appeared in the Times, Daily Telegraph, Countryman, Waterlog, New Writer, New Society (now defunct), Ireland's Own, Scaldy Detail and numerous poetry magazines. Performed writing includes *Revenge*, *The Reluctant Trombonist*, *Send in the Clown* and *Kites and Catullus*. He has read the poems of Seamus Heaney and John Betjeman on BBC television and Shakespeare and Dylan Thomas on BBC radio. Recently he had 12 of his poems published in the anthology *Dust Motes Dancing in the Sunbeams*.

Hear the Colour is Neal's third collection of poetry and follows the widely acclaimed *Turn Now the Tide* (2014) and *Telling It at a Slant* (2013). All are available through major bookstores world-wide and on Amazon. The author has recorded readings of all three publications.

Neal says his life has been shaped by his childhood in North Wales and the Roman town of Colchester, Essex, and – more importantly – by time spent in Ireland, where he now lives. He is divorced and a proud grandparent.

*Hear the colour
see the sound
hunger for
the next blue note*

CONTENTS

Foreword   xi

CALL OF THE WILD

Turn the Wireless Off, You're Waking the Baby!	1
Of Moth and Man	2
Bard's Prayer	3
To a Pipefish	4
War and Peace	6
Red on Blue	9
Big Bang	10
Hedgehog	12
To the Manner Born	13
Those Were the Days	14
Kiln Raiders	15
Cormorant Boy	16
Arrival	18
Word for a Herb	20
Suck of the Sea	21
Begin the Beguine	22
Matterhorn	24
Rowan Berries	25
Knife-in-Water	26
Call of the Wild	28
Plastic Caryatid	31
Yellow	32

HOORAY BOUQUET

Gotcha!	35
Swipsy Cakewalk	36
Soul Survivor	38
Changing of the Light	39
Plato's Not for Jazzin'	40
For Otto	42
On with the Motley	43
Ballet	44
Centurion	45
Hooray Bouquet	46
Silence	49
Va-voom!	50
Passing in the Dark	52
Tramp-Lean	53
Wrap Artist	54
Awakening	55
Onward and Up	56
Biker's Song	58
Last Gasp	60
Fishfall	61
Broken Dream	62
Or Not to Be	64
Really Richard	65
Marathon	66
Knee Play	68
Not Forgot	69
You're Never Alone with a Spider	70
Blue	72

MOTH BALL

Ode to an Old Rose	75
Stars Are Falling Down	76
Drifting	78
Downside-Up	79
No Parallax	80
Trick of Light	81
Reborn on the Fourth of July	82
End of Things to Come	84
Whip-Poor-Will	85
Celyn Valley	88
To a Blackcap	90
Gone but Not Forgot	91
Winter	92
Hell on Earth	93
Moth Ball	94
Hope Hibernal	96
Summer Holiday	97
Mister Pollington	100
Sweet 'Gale	102
Time Cutter	103
Crith of a Heron	104
Silver Adder	106
Boyhood Man	110
Words in Stone	111
Red	112

FOREWORD

In the letters of Ted Hughes, the poet, in the autumn of his years, reflects on a life that, in both tragedy and love, was the equal of any play by the Bard, and concludes, finally, that the only calibration that counts is how much heart people invest, how much they ignore their fears of being hurt or caught out or humiliated. *'And the only thing people regret is that they didn't live boldly enough, that they didn't invest enough heart, didn't love enough. Nothing else really counts at all.'*

It strikes me that Joe Neal is a poet who has never been afraid to love enough and to invest enough heart.

In this collection of finely wrought poems, Joe's third in so many years, there is more evidence of the poetry being as perspicuous as one would expect of prose, or of the economy of journalism, the poet's professional alma mater decades ago, when lines were hammered out on a typewriter in a Fleet Street office in London, infused with the music of the metal keyboard and the rhythm of taut syntax.

I have never believed that the writing of poetry, the summoning of the word or the line or the verse from Karl Jung's collective unconscious, is anything less than mercurial in its conception, protean and mutable, and finally, once out of the womb, like a foal struggling on all fours.

What is remarkable about Joe, with one eye on the inevitable denouement of his great adventure, is his facility with the finesse of a line. His writing is confident. Never flash. Never furnished with the unnecessary or weighted with the spectacular.

There is concision. Clarity. Music. Deliverance. Joe always strikes the right note and, when read aloud, the line delivers, such as *'Alizarin on blue makes me think of you'*, or *'he whistles his delight and dines away the night'*. You can picture the poet at work, emancipating the lines with his classically trained actor's voice, the lilting offspring of Welsh and Wexford currents.

And where do they come from, these lines? With Joe, inspiration is omnipresent – history, the past and present, society – but he digs so unobtrusively that poems, often with little in common, segue harmoniously in an anthology because the poet doesn't unbraid his contribution into minor or major roles. Joe's voice is as distinguishable and as commanding as the blackbird at the gates of dawn.

> *O lead us not*
> *to churchly places*
> *where music reeks of hush*
> *and wide-embracing*
> *lichens measure out*
> *the muted beat of time*

(from 'Bard's Prayer')

There is in Joe's poetry a clear distinction between the poet as a writer and the poet as a musician; I know only too well how important music is in Joe's life, especially jazz, and I have to think that the former card-carrying member of Ronnie Scott's club in Soho, among whose habitués were Lucian Freud and Francis Bacon, knows that creativity is too diverse to be curbed by a single definition.

How you must have twitched
and flailed upon the rock
as searing sun bailed
moisture from your
dwindling tidal strand

(from 'To a Pipefish')

Poets can develop their style by following their ear, which often means surrendering the security that comes from having identifiable parameters to work from and within. To begin at the beginning, each word has a reverberation for a poet of Joe's prescience and sensitivity, and the physical act of labouring the poem into being involves the ordered sound of music and the ordered colour of vision. Rimbaud, for one, believed that each vowel had its own colour.

What I am getting at is that Joe approximates his voice from sources that are distinguishable but have much in common, from size to orthography to tone. Finally, he produces a force of a different hue and style, and what the reader inherits, such as I, is the pleasure of encountering a poem, like a Freud or Bacon portrait, again and again. Enchantment is renewed, and so a fifth or a sixth reading is as exciting and as revealing as the first. The poet, you see, inhabits more than one world, and the poem is the flame of immediate feeling.

I still have my shard
of curving rim
and wonder if I own
the last remaining
jigsaw piece
of amphora to make
Exhibit One complete.

(from 'Kiln Raiders')

Sample poems in this collection like 'War and Peace', 'Hedgehog', 'Cormorant Boy' and 'Plastic Caryatid', and savour not solely Joe's humour and his magpie eye for what continuously glistens in the hall of memory, but how he understands that each single word inhabits more than one universe, which is why we can revisit the poems repeatedly and enjoy them differently. Whoever said it said it best: there is the fire of immediate feeling and lightning illumination among their best properties.

The best guide to Joe's poetry, finally, is Joe himself; only by talking to Joe can you fully engage the universality of his rhythm as a writer of assiduous intent. I was reminded of this recently when I met him after a performance by the great American jazz pianist Eric Reed. Joe's grip on his forthcoming collection – this publication – was that of a tercel. He obsessed minutely about each poem, and what followed was an aura of invisible connotations, and music. Wonderful, infectious company, as you will discover in the pages to follow.

Tom Mooney
June 2015

Call of the Wild

TURN THE WIRELESS OFF, YOU'RE WAKING THE BABY!

Hear the colour,
see the sound,
hunger for
the next blue note;

Ripple-down of yulping sax,
hard-slapped double bass,
knuckled chords,
pedal-pumping thump
and cross-hand stretch
of dis-graced pah-oom stomp;

On this hot night
vowelless rhythm's
king of consonants
as trombone
sticks its brag
in counter-point
to streeling clarinet;

Then starburst fireworks
peal from jubilating
trumpet thrill,
black notes fleeing
the net of beaten time;

Oh man, that's jazz for me!

OF MOTH AND MAN

The red dot creeping slow against the cliff
was smaller than the caterpillar
munching mighty at my feet;

Perspective lent the stripey horn-tailed
creature green giant status as it ate
into the leaves of clinging mountain plant;

With scope I watched the figure grope a ledge
defying the placing of his feet – knowing
grub will make a moth, he himself a man.

BARD'S PRAYER

O lead us not
to churchly places
where music reeks of hush
and wide-embracing
lichens measure out
the muted beat of time;

Let us go instead
to gaze at turbulence
of water as it spurtles
over rock, pounding stone
to beds of grit –
whence spawning fish
can cycle life again.

Hear the Colour

TO A PIPEFISH

How you must have twitched
and flailed upon the rock
as searing sun bailed
moisture from your
dwindling tidal strand;

How your pouting mouth
must have sucked
and puffed to push
and siphon water through
those fluttering
filaments of gill;

How you must have fought
to stay upright in your
eelgrass habitat as the sea
that held you seeped away;

And how you were left
to lie in wait for your
horizontal, gasping death.

Thus I found you,
high and dry, beyond
the succour of the waves,
still so elegant
in your elongated form;

Call of the Wild

And now you adorn
my mantel shelf,
hard and brittle,
grey as dust,
a little life force spent.

Hear the Colour

WAR AND PEACE

You said you were my father,
the man in the khaki coat,
and let me pull
the trigger of your gun:

A Lee-Enfield .303
– I know that now,
used to kill the enemy
far across the sea,
while I was home
in Wales with Mum.

I called you Daddy –
and I remember that you cried,
silently,
as snow fell on your head.

Six years you fought
in drenching mud
and other people's blood
– kill or they'll kill you,
a do-or-die machine
whose pity had no place to be;

A sergeant-major, raging
for his men,
you watched as Stukas strafed

Call of the Wild

fleeing French refugees
and held a dying child,
hurling hatred
at the parting plane.

You struggled with the family
you later raised,
and measured peace
against the war
that tore
you from the comfort
clutch of pastures green;

Suffer little children
you could not –
humanity had died
in you, like the sapping
life you'd cradled
in your rage
against that awful,
frowning sky.

But hate within
could not survive
the oxygen of love
our mother breathed
for us, and music
you staccato-played
in cavalcade of colour
out of black and white
re-made the man
we all called Dad.

Hear the Colour

Thus I recollect
the only time
you really laughed –
pounding your piano
in the parlour;

And, tethered
to the honky-tonk of fun,
two brothers and their mum.

Call of the Wild

RED ON BLUE

Alizarin
on blue
makes me
think
of you
in deckchair
days
when
relaxing
was such fun;
side by side
I seemed
so wan,
but you
belonged
astride
the sun!

Hear the Colour

BIG BANG

Explosions are what make me tick;
ideally that's how I'd like to go
if fate decreed the knowledge
of our time of death – no bits,
no funeral, just complete
disintegration; dust unto dust
– literally, a drink or two
to celebrate (or denigrate)
a life of scant significance.

Now, next to smell of breaking waves
or yellow gorse in sunshine
after rain, spent gunpowder
gives me that madeleine thrill
of recollection that Proust
banged on about so elegantly.

It all began, this strange love
of detonation, on a beach
in Wales when two boys found
a wartime unexploded mine;
throwing stones at it only made
it clang – we had to hit its horns
point-on to generate a bang,
so instead we rolled a boulder
down the steepest bank, and fled.

Call of the Wild

The silence, when it hit, confused
us then – so we two brothers sneaked
a look from behind our safety nook
in time to hear a rumbling roar
as debris rose into the sky;
beside my hands that held my head
there fell a jagged piece of iron
that would have had me dead.

We ran for it and never stopped
until we'd reached the road;
oh, to hear that bang again and see
the hole the powder dug – instead
of tearing ships apart in time
of war when bombs were set
to kill, not boys to entertain!

Hear the Colour

HEDGEHOG

'Thrice and once
the hedgepig whined'
– so said the Second Witch,
and dire it was,
the consequence;
but when my spikey
friend comes snuffling
round the slug-crept
cabbage patch,
he whistles his delight
and dines away the night,
oblivious to death's knock
should he stray
onto the motorway.

TO THE MANNER BORN

The style they'd chosen
for the decor of the room
was a nod to neo-classical baroque
– though the daughter of the house,
who'd offered me the student job
of painting it, was proving
far less willing than the nymphs
that Bacchus chased across the ceiling.

For soon I was to know
that if you didn't have
that touch of class
enjoyed by privilege,
you needn't chance your arm;
still I had the work and earned
my crust to supplement the grant
I'd lost in a bluffing poker game.

Two lessons learned: stick
to who and what you know
and keep your place where you belong,
and so I write and act
and play the fool a bit
with my trombone; I wonder what
she did with her exotic life
– not that Bacchus gives a stuff!

Hear the Colour

THOSE WERE THE DAYS

Duffel coats and skiffle groups
and Humph at the Hundred Club;
jazz at Eel Pie Island
and bop at Ronnie Scott's;
fumbled whirls with older girls
in sixth-form holidays;
earnings saved for Soho
nights and spent instead on drink;
jukebox cellar coffee bars
and Godot at the Vic;
Olivier blacked-up to play
the Moor and Burton
getting drunk; blue-eyed O'Toole
rides out of desert sun;
Profumo caught with Keeler
and Rockers fight the Mods;
Doctor Who comes flying through
… then Kennedy's shot dead.

Call of the Wild

KILN RAIDERS

When we were picking
stones to help prepare
the playing fields,
we boys and girls found
pottery and green-aged
coins with Caesar's head
staring from a distant
past of Roman occupation.

Of course, we pocketed
our plundered trove
before museum people
came to dig the spot,
uncovering a kiln
where Marcus, Gaius
or Octavius had turned
and thumbed a wheel
of clay and baked a pot.

I still have my shard
of curving rim
and wonder if I own
the last remaining
jigsaw piece
of amphora to make
Exhibit One complete.

CORMORANT BOY

Somewhere, in Ireland, there stands a rock ...

No words he ever heard
or spoke – the awkward,
gangly boy, taunted
for his hearing loss.

He spends the days away
from bruising human company,
finding kinship
with the kinder ways of nature.

In silent, solitary walks
he senses all about him
and sees and feels
what noisy people miss.

One day he happens on a cave
behind a waterfall and wonders
at the gauze of mist that shuts
him from the world he left.

Ahead he scrapes his way
through tunnels in the rock
until a light before
reveals a shelf above the sea.

Call of the Wild

Now he sits there, staring
at the sun – darkened silhouette
among cormorants who bring fish
and leave them at his feet.

For centuries, they say,
he's kept a vigil from the ledge;
buachaíll cailleach dhubh
they call the rock.

I'll take you there
if you dare to brave
the waterfall like
that lonely cormorant boy.

And if you listen,
you can hear
the speaking waves
as they well against the cliff:

Buachaíll cailleach dhubh,
buachaíll cailleach dhubh ...

ARRIVAL

In prowling dream
I came upon my hamlet home
with a suddenness
of dawning fireball sun
– where sad tarmac ends
and cobbles mark
the start of history.

Bent-faced houses
beckoned, mellow brick
like bark upon
a Scots pine tree
– just waiting
to be rubbed by me.

Here, town-raised
country folk,
gentrified
in conversation,
debate between
themselves about
longevity of lavender
and monster marrow
breeding compost
that feeds the smell
of roses – so have

Call of the Wild

a cup of tea,
my dear, and join
us on the lawn.

No thanks, I'm bored
with this; mountains
beckon me – back
where I was born.

WORD FOR A HERB

Herb Robert,
you are such
a plucky
little plant,
adorning
meanest place
with pink trace
petals and rufous
leaves and stem.

And what a call
to arms is your
scintillating smell!
No pulling punches
with such pugilistic
pungencies
in corners
where you dwell.

Herb you are for sure
– very much a Robert,
not a Bob –
proud to grow in grotty
common spot,
adding dignity
and character
where other
plants do not.

Call of the Wild

SUCK OF THE SEA

Lashes of rock cut through the froth waves,
kinks in the current to hazard the brave
who hanker for herrings that shoal in the sea

ta-rarara-ree, ta-rarara-ree

About the ship comes in haul of the net,
slap to the swell as keel drags on weed,
tilting the decks in suck to and fro

ta-rarara-ro, ta-rarara-ro

Then, with a snap, bow breaks free of the pull
and gouges a path through dull of the trough
to shudder to safety, the hulk and her crew

ta-rarara-roo, ta-rarara-roo

Hear the Colour

BEGIN THE BEGUINE

Here we are again –
earwigs crowding in,
pinching naked skin
and flighting
to the light.

This year's global
warming pleasure
is a happy glut
of Painted Lady
butterflies
– stopping off
from Africa
to flutter colour
at my greening
valley home;

Then streaming trail
of Orange Tips,
hatchlings seeking
sun by sparkling
beds of watercress
– my spring
has just begun;

Multi-coloured
beetle thuds

Call of the Wild

into the kitchen
from pine-tree habitat
– Harlequin by name,
bug to raise a grin
in me, performer
unrestrained in such
bright company;

But back to little
earwig, seen breaking
out of winter egg
laid months before
on hearthside log
– nymph ghostly white
in transparentness,
spreading darker
like a spill of ink
from pincer tail
through segments
to antennae head.

New life begins
and I quite forget
a nip that drew my blood.

Hear the Colour

MATTERHORN

No other mountain
casts a shadow
on the sky
as well as on the snow below;

No other profile
of a peak
so tattoos
the meniscus of the mind;

No other rock
spells death
and invincibility
in such seductive silhouette;

And in zesty Zermatt
crouched below
ice picks rust and mark
the final rest of those who were rebuffed.

ROWAN BERRIES

Tiny clumps of treasure
dangling from a thread,
just waiting to be picked
but first sift them
through your fingers,
weigh them in the hand,
knead them,
count them if you can;
a blind man doesn't
know their colour
but wills them
to be bright;
not quite orange,
nor yet red –
vermilion, I'd have said.

KNIFE-IN-WATER

Better that instead
of his compulsive whim
to hurl a penknife
riverwards, Goethe
used its many blades
to trim the compound
ripple words the German
nation's drowning in.

His toss-up choice,
if he saw the splash,
was to stay a writer
– if not, a painter be;
but fate was sealed
by a willow tree.

Later on he was to write:

'Gathered in the
poet's pure hand
the waters will
congeal.'

Now that knife lies
beneath the silt,
safe in the bosom
of the Rhine –

as are his wisdom words,
clutched in time sublime.

> *Goethe described how he used the splash of his penknife – hurled into the Rhine on a whim – to decide whether to give up painting and concentrate on being a writer. He heard the splash but didn't see the knife's entry because of an over-hanging willow. The sound was enough. His mind had already been made up!*

Hear the Colour

CALL OF THE WILD

Mooncalf moan
of my blown trombone
tells cats Caenwen
that it's feeding time;

Sackbut sounds
riff through the vale
with promise
of meat from a tin;

But no food
that I buy
will make them deny
their lust
for a natural kill;

Squirrel and shrew,
robins and wrens
– even my hens –
are fair game
for siblings
who bear the same name;

Assassins in tandem
they are – but by giving
a home to two kittens
alone I knew not what
horrors I'd bring;

Call of the Wild

Now that they've gone,
grown old and moved on,
the rats have returned
– no longer a snack
for identi-kit cat.

***

Jazz-fed chickens
in fol-de-rol
prefer the sax
for cookhouse call;

Its soprano tone
has them fly
to the door –
and if it's ajar,
they'll land
on the floor,
pook-pook-pooking
at Panama Rag;

That's a Plenty
sets egg-lay mood,
then, sax aside,
a trombone slide
evicts them
from the kitchen
– to resume their
free-range romp;

And Chauntecleer
halloos his hens

Hear the Colour

with Pathé News
performance
doodle-doos.

Call of the Wild

PLASTIC CARYATID

Skills absorbed in execution of a sketch
of Athens' beautiful Erechtheion
match spills of ink, artist's spraint consumed
by ancient marble step – student tourist's
blemish on gamboge stone of Parthenon,
there for the next millennium or two.

Finished drawing then was parcelled up and sent
with love, and Hellenic stamp, to a girl
called Jen, crafted from afar (Caryatid
third from left) in Winsor Newton tint
that brimmed with shining black affection.

But it didn't last: I'd moved on – like always,
drawn by thoughts of greener grass behind the hill
– until, years on with all my options gone,
I too now languish like a plastic
memory in a case of glass, alone
and looked at but no longer stirring hearts.

> *Sadly, I own to spilling Indian ink on the steps of the Parthenon; the original Caryatids, maidens holding up the roof, were later moved to the Acropolis museum to escape being eaten by the acid air. Plastic replicas now take the strain.*

Hear the Colour

YELLOW

Headless dandelions,
undandied
by the wind,
stand tall
against clipped grass
while seed fluff
twirls away
to grow the colour
once again;

Nature's quantitative
easing keeps
the dazzle tint
in front of petals pink
and purple, red and blue
– and gets the vote
of insects too;

Yes, yellow tops
the pollinating
pops with bees
that give a suck.

HOORAY BOUQUET

Hooray Bouquet

GOTCHA!

Cuckooed in his plundered
whelken habitat,
the hermit crab
waits upon the tide,
big claw held
aloft like triumph
in the boxing ring;
look out, they'd say
if shrimps could yell,
here comes Diogenes
– that moving
mountain of a shell!

Hear the Colour

SWIPSY CAKEWALK

When you rang I was washing
my trombone;
in seventh position and slide
right out, it just fits the bath.

Suds in the bell,
then rinse with gel,
rub down and dry,
then polish it well.

Time for a tune;
what will it be? Careless Love
– played in C?

What's that you say?
Either me or my trombone?
Let's see:
okay, you go. I'll blow.

So now I'm Nobody's Sweetheart;
didn't we have A Fine Romance?
All right, I promise: There'll Be
Some Changes Made.

I see, you want All Of Me;
must I really play Bye Bye Blues?
You used to love Swipsy Cakewalk,
and what about One O'Clock Jump?

Hooray Bouquet

Okay, I know, I'm just
a Big Butter And Egg Man.
You know what, you're just
a Hard Hearted Hannah!

Why don't you Come On
And Stomp, Stomp, Stomp?
Surely Our Love
Is Here To Stay?

Must I Sit Right Down
And Write Myself A Letter?
Am I just a Stranger
On The Shore?

You say you've
had too much
of Blues My Naughty
Sweety Gives To Me.

But isn't that
the Glory Of Love?
Now I Don't Get Around
Much Anymore.

SOUL SURVIVOR

I know someone
who lives alone
and visit him
from time to time;

We talk of memories
akin to both of us
– of people loved
and those unmet;

Of places seen
or glimmers in a dream
we shared on this,
our alter-ego trip.

Hooray Bouquet

CHANGING OF THE LIGHT

The sun is changing colour, perceptions
are evolving like ripples in the air,
ultra-ultra wavelengths elongating
beauty beyond the wit of physicists.

Listen, you can hear the shades of yellow
murmur in the brightness of the light,
morphing into orange then relaxing
to a red you've never seen before.

Just you wait until the night when moon
is mooding blue again and stars cast
shadows like violet violations
of all the lore we've come to understand.

Hear the Colour

PLATO'S NOT FOR JAZZIN'

So let us nail
the ambiguity in Plato's
labyrinthine sway
when he tells of rhythm
being the path
to harmony –
unless you measure
pace of step
towards the bliss
of love on love;

But then the Roman
soul Catullus,
a man with three
beats to his name,
would be better
placed to spell
that sullen art
in perfect poet time.

Now back to age
of Plato lest we
classically digress:
in Athens the word
is less, not more,
when you wish

Hooray Bouquet

to make your mark
– to impress
the minds around you
in scholar's argument.

To boil it down:
two harmonies
allowed in life,
says Mister P,
one the strain
of courage,
the other temperance.

Today G minor fits
the bill; no place
for the thump
and bleat of jazz
(pleasure just for
pleasure's sake) –
oh no, the ancient's
mind would blow!

FOR OTTO

Side by side on Father's
wide piano stool they sat,
crossing hands to grab
each other's keys –
crotchets, quavers
ricocheting the night
away in post-war
pacificity;

Dad and Otto,
his pub-found friend,
ex-POW from Camp 186
– alchemists making jazz
across the lines,
putting war to peace:
sergeants both who fought
for lands they loved.

Hooray Bouquet

ON WITH THE MOTLEY

When we first met you were wearing banded
Mott the Hoople socks like all young dudes
and twirling down the street to glam rock beat
of Steve Harley singing 'Make me smi-ile'.

We held hands and walked the whoopsie-do
– and now look at you, standing there bewigged,
defeminised, berating witnesses
in your courtly clothes of black and white,
consigning other people's muddled lives
to pink-tied bundled words of evidence.

When your prosecution's done, do put on
the glam, come up and see me, make me smile.

Again.

BALLET

Silent figures
relishing their space
assume immobile
picture presence
on the stage.

Blue-note tenor
saxophone punctuates
the modularity of theme
as rhythm postulates
movement yet to come.

The dance begins
– abruptly.

Hooray Bouquet

CENTURION

The hand that skims the stone is not my own
as I stand and watch by Dinas Lake,
and why the shadow when there is no sun?

Across the other side was once a camp
where Romans tried to tame the wild of Wales
and, alone, a dreaming sentry skimmed a stone.

Melting ice sheets rub and squeak on rock
as wind shoals eeling ripples underneath
– but why the shadow when there is no sun?

Centurion, your mind was home in Rome
with warmth and grapes – not frozen winterland,
downing spear to skim a foreign stone.

Puzzle shapes no longer fit as breeze-blown
corrugations drive the thaw along,
but why the shadow when there is no sun?

And here I am, two thousand years along,
watching still by Snowdon's bitten brow;
the hand that skims the stone is not my own
– and why the shadow when there is no sun?

Hear the Colour

HOORAY BOUQUET

Lines written to a poorly patient in lieu of a bunch of flowers.

For mood of persiflage,
choose the saxifrage
– jupiters of pink
and blue and white,
clinging to the ground
and rooting
for the quench
of gentle rain –
as is the way
of a little xerophyte.

For jubilation, I'd go
for yellow gorse
– sweet smells
of coconut
in pod-pop beat of sun.

Then those sleepy
nights with digitalis
purpurea (that's foxglove
to you and me)
making hearts
go diddly-dee,

Hooray Bouquet

slyly nodding
you to bed with red
and purple head –
all the while ignoring
petal trails of indigo
forget-me-nots.

In morning flight again,
run you down by clumps
of bogland willowherb
and honeyed woodbine droop
where brilliant hawkmoths
hide their beauty,
flashing in the dark.

But thyme is of the essence,
wind-tousled tang of sheepen
pastureland, as you step
towards the sea;
rock rose, purslane
– you're assaulted
by the salted scents.

Turning back to town,
past sagging bindweed
hedge, pause to watch
the splaw-legged
waddle of a silent rook,
safe from guns
on treeless tarmac land.

Hear the Colour

Then through the gate
to that familiar
pathway home,
cobbles leading
to the door
and rose-trooped
colours marking
patient's safe return.

So now you have
beside the bed
a jar of thoughts;
hear the colour,
glimpse the frankincense,
connect to pain-free
days of zestfulness
– and get well soon!

SILENCE

Emptiness
that follows
the passing
of a train;
the clack
of woodquest
wings in night
rest settlement;
long pause
in Pinter
play on radio;
paranoia poised
between two
plopping drips;
impossible
to grasp,
all this,
with sound
of tinnitus.

Hear the Colour

VA-VOOM!

Smoke on water,
snow on sun

dah-dah-dahrrr
dah-dah-dah-dahrrr

The bassline riffs
have just begun

But ragtime's
just the opposite

With stride piano
it's the pah-oom sound

Swaggered chords
puffed up like a cloud

Yes, rhythm was king
with Jelly Roll
and cross-hand Fats

Pumping pedal to celebrate
the din that made us bounce
at Waller's whim

A Handful Of Keys,
that's what the Harlem
Fuss was all about

Hooray Bouquet

We rode the rocket
then – music now
is not a stomp on him

dah-dah-dahrrr
dah-dah-dah-dahrrr
dah-dah-dah-dah-dahrrr

– or is it … ?

PASSING IN THE DARK

Squinting at her crystal ball,
the frazzled gypsy fixed me
with her crooked stare
and said, 'The tragedy of life
is yearned-for love
unmet by reciprocity –
the tunnel dug from different
ends that never makes the link.'

Then she opened wide
her arms and said, 'It happens
to us all, and happen
we to it; think now
of countless diggings –
journeys struck in parallel,
stuck straight
in single track.'

With this she loosed
a single tear
and watched it fall
and trickle round
the glinting globe of glass.
'All we need to do,'
she said, 'is bend it
– just a little bit.'

Hooray Bouquet

TRAMP-LEAN

It was the way he slept, with one hand
pointing heavenwards, that caught the eye
– not so much the man with warm skull face
who slumbered on with empty bottle
by his boney side that angled on the seat;

No, it was how he leant with such content
– 'tramp-lean' would make a handy title
to the picture as a work of art –
and in that sleep what dreams might come?
Perfection in another place
denied to him by paltry circumstance?

I watched him for a while and then became
concerned lest he should be no more alive,
'til he startled up in flailing agitation
sending bottle rolling down the street
– his accusing finger pointing after it.

WRAP ARTIST

Your paper always wrapped
my stone
in games we played alone;
I remember
this each time I see
the hate
that straddles love
when nations
break the scissor power
to cut;
no, words placate and end
the enmity
– like the little
crosses
you once wrote to me.

Hooray Bouquet

AWAKENING

Sad eyes said to me:

Ride the rainbow then
– but know that milk
for babes and meat
for adulthood are dark
sayings forgot with age
when other nourishment
takes precedence
and early bent to wiser
ways melts like wax
in haughty aspiration;

With earthward slide
you'll realise
the black-read book
funds divinity
in ordinary man
– proverbially.

> *Prompted by thoughts on Blake's 'dark sayings' – the heavy metaphors, the 'black' hidden meanings within the Book of Proverbs.*

Hear the Colour

ONWARD AND UP

Parting at the estuary
was such bleak sorrow
for you and me –
dirged by eisteddfodau
of scoter, grebe and guillemot
and clarinetting oyster bird.

Turning to the mightiness
of rising rock for strength
to carry on alone,
I hunched into the wind
and yomped away the misery,
ouzel-piped aboard
a mountain floating
in the drift of mist.

Following the white-bibbed
darkling thrush (dodging
screes and crags
in jouncing furtiveness),
I pressed past snow-stilled
frozen mops of scrub
– and forgot we'd ever met.

Arriving, ouzel-led
before the rising jut,

Hooray Bouquet

I found a cave
to shiver through
my nightfall purgatory.

Taking soundings then
to meet the sun
(feet in thousands,
on and up – ETA
the dawning day),
I saw my life a climb
apart from yours,
ready to be drawn astray.

> *The ring ouzel is a bird of the mountain; its piping call*
> *and flight of hide-and-seek among the rocks can lead*
> *you on and up.*

Hear the Colour

BIKER'S SONG

When you walked
into the water
you left
your footprints
in the sand;

When we rode
astride the Harley
I felt you
pressing
from behind;

When we swayed
to take the corner
you hugged
me tightly
with your hands;

And we sang our song
together,
riding on our minds:

Hang-a-left astride a Harley
focus eyes upon the sky

Hang-a-right astride a Harley
see the country rolling by

Hooray Bouquet

When they dragged
you from the waves
they smudged
those footprints
with your heels;

But I know
you are still
with me
as I ride
the same two wheels:

Hang-a-right astride a Harley
see the country rolling by

Hang-a-left astride a Harley
focus eyes upon the sky

Share the joy of being together
with a Harley on your mind

LAST GASP

Smoking was a fun thing once,
cigarettes with names
like Turf and Strand
and State Express,
but often I would puff
a glowing pipe tamped down
with shag cut rough,
clamping teeth on noble
curving stem, bow-tie man
in check sports coat
– at seventeen saying
'whizzo' like a bomber
pilot back from busting
up a dam; the Rolling
Stones and Beatles
ruled the day,
but I bucked the trend –
student old before his time,
cultivating image even then.

Hooray Bouquet

FISHFALL

The rod man treads dainty by the river,
a shadow chasing fishfall in the night;
he knows not where he'll cast his baited hook
until he hears circumnutating plop,
ripples purged of all baroque, as trout from sea
sucks in a fly off gliding surface skim;
it's there, in moonsplash, that he'll wait until
the water parts again and he can guess
at grub he'll match with pattern tied by him;
and so it is, in life, when we do seek
that hidden chance of catching happiness.

BROKEN DREAM

I found you magpied
in the mess that is my house
– nudging mounted moths
and birds' eggs blown
two centuries ago
by nature's genteel terrorists;
and embrangled in the mithe
of bric-a-brac – tinplate
wind-up toys in yellow,
red and blue, snuggled
up with lead farm animals
and ticking fishing
reels and hooks
and weights and flies
to fool the river fish;
and there you were
– my Denis Compton
cricket bat, signed
by him and bearing
marks of balls I hit
for six; but woodworm's
got you now, for when
I took you for a slog
with neighbour bowling
down the garden lawn,
you broke in half

Hooray Bouquet

– one memory too far
for manhood boy trapped
in self-made warp of time.

Hear the Colour

OR NOT TO BE

The sun is young
and moon grown old
– day has just begun;
red squirrels chew
the cones of lime-green
larch, grasping
daintily while
keeping wary eye
for marten predator;

By rushy stream below,
a dipper curtsies
on a rock –
plucking snails
from trailing weed;

And from a branch
of oak by broken
bridge above,
a darkened form
hangs twisting
in the wind
– toil of life
too great to bear
on a morning
just begun.

Hooray Bouquet

REALLY RICHARD

Car parks usurping history,
Wars of Roses and lost causes;
old bones of a warrior king,
kudos in cathedral places
– battleground for teeming tourists;
no horse now, no Yorkist
crowndom in Elizabethan time
– but buried life rehabilitated,
for Richard was a kindly man,
much put upon by little princes
and the words of William S
– a story of identity
with a spinal twist.

Hear the Colour

MARATHON

Gulled on by shrieking fantasies, I pound
the streets in aweful honour of the Greeks;
body moves in ways approved by Spartan
man – automatically, without heed of pain;
thoughts whip the spirit into fear of shame
– sixteen miles still to be accounted for
and legs pleading for yet another
layer of disdain to bury deeper
in sweaty swaddlement of comfort zone.

Hit the Road Jack – not my name but the song
will do for this hilly bit to come;
'I wasted time and now doth time waste me' –
Shakespeare's Richard Two comes into mind,
something about 'numbering clock'
(good one, that – I'll save the dungeon scene for later);
colours coming now … on a beach somewhere:
a misty rain blowing off the water
and a dying sun has begun to paint

a rainbow across the sky, just the hint
of one, with its left foot set gently down
among the houses of a little town;
looking out to sea, I glimpse the other
end of the spectrum's arch – then, as if
at the flick of a switch, the whole curve lights

Hooray Bouquet

the leaden sky with its seven glorious
hues, linking land to a magic mark
on the sea's impossible horizon.

Nearly there, I think, clinging to that sky
where to the west, sandwiched 'twixt silver
stratus and the spikey marram profile
of the dunes, pleated piles of wispy
cumulus glow oxslip yellow, turning,
at the stroke of a brush, through burnished
gold to hectic orange and cerise;
now I see a curlew pass across
the glowing canvas, its down-curved bill

and feathers disco-tinted by the blood
filled sky – 'kourlie, kourlie, kourlie' –
wistful, bubbling cry cueing in the night,
but first come climactic pinks and mauves …
Is that Charon waiting with his boat? Pay
the ferryman? Not me. Now I cannot see
at all – but I can hear my feet beating
up the street (or is it just the rhythm
of my heart?). Am I there? Is it over yet?

Hear the Colour

KNEE PLAY

Counting down
to yesterday,
light years fly by
– meeting Einstein
in the sky.

Beach walker
staring at the sea
– crunching numbers,
squaring MC
in ecstasy of E.

Interloper of my dream
– speaking solfège
tongues to me
that I may see
sense in all of This
that now is That

in the knee play
of a life that was.

> *Thoughts provoked by the timeless experience of Philip Glass's opera with its running narratives of 'knee-play' intermezzos.*

NOT FORGOT

Hooked cup waits
suspended
on the wall;

Mouse mess mingles
with the peppercorn
in un-pestled
mortar pot;

Cold chimney
draws down
the sooted wind,
riffing corner
of the rug
against the chair
she chuckled in.

She's passed
into the past;
remember her
as the cottage
does – in sounds
familiar.

Hear the Colour

YOU'RE NEVER ALONE WITH A SPIDER

I call her Ida,
my six-legged spider;
you see, I checked her out
in my arachnid book
and know she's of the fairer sex;
but how she lost two
shapely legs she cannot tell.

With four one side and two
the other, she cuts a dashing
curve across the floor and ends
up near her starting point,
where she waits awhile
to regain strength for yet
another paralympic scurry.

Thinking it's the bathroom
that she wants – and a sip
of water from the tub –
I place a saucer within
six paces of her
reluctant-insect form and wait.

Two hours later she's still
standing there, and the saucer's dry.

Did she take a lick
while I wasn't looking?

Hooray Bouquet

Or did the water
just evaporate?
Like with the missing
legs, I'll never know for sure
– but this is what I think
about her accident:

One giant step it took
to pin my spider to the floor,
but she gamely struggled
free, losing two limbs
above the hairy knee.
Little wonder, then,
that she's reluctant
to court more danger
from this human stranger.

Each day I find her
in the room, I count
my blessings – and hers too,
and yearn to see her grow
another pair;
but she's no regenerating
worm and, besides,
I wouldn't know her then.

So I speak to her
and hope that little
by little my Ida
will learn a spider
trust of me;
my voice, her silence,
what a perfect combination!

Hear the Colour

BLUE

Hear my colour,
it sings in blue
– harmonics
of my love for you;
words divide,
tones unite,
cobalt eyes
strike chords
that ring accord
between us both
in azure, indigo
and cyan
combination;
now blink,
think deepest sea
– find infinity.

MOTH BALL

Moth Ball

ODE TO AN OLD ROSE

All dead roses should be dyed;
what do you think now,
what will you think then?

Just look: perplexed petals
drooling off the stem;
gone is the corolla
of concupiscence,
once pinkly deliquescent
now darkly dehydrated,
shuddering at the caress of rain.

But if you try to represent
this indignity of fading life,
you find in each charred line
and deeply darkened shade
a noble belligerence
which shimmers with a sense
of what has gone before.

So look down the stem
and see again another rose
still closed on beauty yet to come.

Hear the Colour

STARS ARE FALLING DOWN

Shooting stars are falling on the mountain,
dropping just before the blush of dawn
– so the shepherd says;
and as the day draws on, downcast curlew
calls across the crag, flagging rain to come.

Along the cliffs, acrobatic choughs,
in tumbling flash of red and black, pretend
to clumsiness of flight
– watched by leaping goats, not to be outdone
in their display of ledge-hop derring-do.

All these things he sees, one man and his dog
leading scattered sheep to less sparse grass
sheltered from the wind;
he knows each one of them and sheds a tear
if fluke or adder bite should take its toll.

In time of halcyon he identifies
the butterflies and flowers and curling ferns
that hide in modesty;
but tadpole spawn that dollops in the wet,
he thinks, is rot of meteorites that fall

down in the night – for how can frogs leap up
a wild Welsh peak to join his bleating sheep?
No, the word is out:

Moth Ball

shooting stars are falling on the mountain,
dropping just before the blush of dawn.

>*In Wales, frogspawn on a mountain is called* pydru ser
>*– rot of the stars.*

DRIFTING

When I have that flying dream
it's always Persia where I've been,
but Naishápúr is not a scene
where modern 'scrapers touch the sky;

No, it's Khayyám's call of eastern peace
with minarets and blossom trees
and bustle of the market place
– and ruby vintage drink and thee and me;

Now, adrift in waking time,
I'm lost in space,
astronaut alone in bowl of night
– journeying, never seeing the light.

Moth Ball

DOWNSIDE-UP

Walk the mountain
tread the snow
thrust with feet
stand at ninety with the contour of the peak

Turn in rhythm of a pendulum
carve the ice
press and sway in ecstasy
leap the slope with brief control of destiny

Know the way to ski

Hear the Colour

NO PARALLAX

I see, in parallax, a finning fish
and know he's not quite where my mind perceives
his place to be;
so is it when your wanton words conceal
the truth from me;
mostly the expression on your face tells
the story that you seek to obfuscate;
but still, in love,
I choose to take the far-fetched message
that you formulate
– believing it, the wide-eyed way, like
a bornly child startled by the life-light.

TRICK OF LIGHT

Abracadabra
mountain
dawn,
magenta
scrawl
of lips
and tongue,
rocky profile
mouths at
thrusting
sun,
buoyed up
through sky
of buttermilk
– the day
has just begun.

Hear the Colour

REBORN ON THE FOURTH OF JULY

Thoughts stirred by found chess pieces carved from a wooden leg in Boston, Mass.

When Washington came
to inspect the caught men
– maimed prisoners of war –
he ordered them treated
as equal to all other folk.

'Who's this, then?' pointing
to Sam. 'Lootenant is he,
one of King George's marines.'

'Leftenant,' said Sam, for
that was his name.

'Lootenant we say in the US of A;
you're now in a country that's free.
You'll get a new leg,
we've good wood growing here.'

'Thank you,' said Sam,
'but my ship's made of oak.'

'So be it,' said Washington George.
'You're welcome to stay,
moored by your leg

Moth Ball

in this country of ours
– and soon when you're well
you must come and take tea
with my family and me.'

'I never drink tea.
Lootenants drink gin,'
said Sam with a grin.

And so Sam Foster he stayed
and became one of them
in a life that he'd lead
for sixty years more.

When in his last days,
lying infirm in the bed,
he carved from his leg
chess pieces to play
– life skilled and fulfilled,
for that was his way.

Hear the Colour

END OF THINGS TO COME

My love, you are the scratch that feeds the itch,
so tickle me the more lest I forget
to notice when you turn towards the door,

for passions are the end of things to come.

Anoint me with the blood that stained the sword
from wrath you felt for me the day you left,

for passions are the end of things to come.

Now you're back again, we can concentrate
on being the one that's stronger than the two
that slew our fragile joy the first time round,

for passions are the end of things to come.

Moth Ball

WHIP-POOR-WILL

The call of New Hampshire State.

In dreams you find
you're moving
further west
– from Wales
and Wexford, Ireland,
to Winnipesaukee,
from mountain
bordered sea
to island scattered
lake: Wyeths
on the wall,
scrimshaw in glass
case – and Audubon
peregrine in print;

Harley bikers like
it too – bandana-bright
in convoy, riding
head upright,
where laws say
'helmets optional'
and roadside
boulder-crushers
make mincemeat

Hear the Colour

of the past,
on Highway 28;

Look now, across
mud-snow road:
that clapboard house,
faced away
from brink of rock,
blowing log-fire
smoke from stack
the swifts
will nestle in
when warmer winds
from south and west
hustle in the spring
and White Mountain
sheds its melt;

Then, monarch
butterflies,
black-etched
on red, add
brightness
to a sickly sun,
soon to kindle
up to ninety
Fahrenheit;

And in those warmer
nights, fireflies
prick the purple

Moth Ball

comfort of the air
– and stoop awaits
with lime and gin
as whip-poor-will
speaks for creatures
from the wood
and ghost-call
lakeside loons
caress you
into wakefulness;

Live free or die,
the motto says,
in this the Granite
State you're in.

Hear the Colour

CELYN VALLEY

Sometimes nature's flooding rains can claim
a whole community and life will never
be the same again;
but for man to drown a thriving village
deliberately – not with bouncing bomb
in time of war, but when church is full
of song and people talk and get along –
that's beyond the pale.

And yet it happened to a peaceful place
called Capel Celyn just fifty years ago;
eight hundred acres
of productive land, twelve farms, a chapel,
school and post office – and livelihoods
of people too – all to fill a reservoir
for strangers far away.

Gone are homes with names like Tynybont
and Dol and Penbryn Fawr – and a farm
where early Quakers
met in glow-worm light of valley night –
and a Welsh-speaking village which kept its
culture in the face of changing time;
now tombstone names swim wet in double death
decreed by Albion.

Moth Ball

In memory of a North Wales village, its history and its people, sacrificed to supply the water needs of another nation. Never again – byth eto.

TO A BLACKCAP

Twenty feet from where I sleep
she sits to hatch her eggs;
her nest is such a skimpy thing,
hanging hammocked from the bendy
branches of a fuchsia hedge.

It is my privilege
to host this little bird
who chose sanctuary
with me in preference
to the alder carr below.

Blackcap, you are an honoured
guest – so regale me
with your warbled song
to celebrate the swelling
madrigal *fortissimo*.

Moth Ball

GONE BUT NOT FORGOT

I knew you once and now you're species dead
– crossed off the list of Linnaeus, named
in Latin by lepidopterists
who marvelled at your exotic life.

Large Blue your name in English, scarce enough
when as a boy I took you in my net
– just to see your rarity, brightest
butterfly where colour matched the sky.

And then I let you go and watched you fly
into the summer sun, not knowing then
how odd your life began – caterpillar
feeding on the buds of thyme, then grabbed

by stinging ants and drawn down into
hummock nest beneath, and there your segment
gland of sweetness milked by teeming brood
who gave you food of tiny, squirming grub.

Pupating, one year on, you hatched to be
the handsome butterfly I used to see –
before you came to be extinct, now pinned
and labelled in that cabinet of time.

The Large Blue butterfly became extinct in 1979.

WINTER

Pulsing transpiration
slows in sky-stretch
staunch of trees;
abscission shrugs
the terminated
leaf adrift;
snowfall's compline
bell calls prayer
for pristine sleep,
proclaiming countdown
to spring's resurrection
– that rhapsody in green.

Moth Ball

HELL ON EARTH

A people pounded by religion
cannot fit the boot of a foreign state
– however hard the cobbler drives the nail;
forced democracy has its ghoulish
consequence in evil caliphate
where distortion of belief dooms
half a continent to devil's drool
in death-on-death for suffering's sake.

Now only more the same can end the game
of torture, flags and funny walks;
against all this the rest of us measure
out our lot in pitiful irrelevance,
selling souls so willingly to crude,
blaspheming reality TV.

Hear the Colour

MOTH BALL

Shunning mask of darkness,
star-bright seething shapes
congregate on moonwash
white of wall: Eyed Hawk
partners plum-brown Lappet
in the moth ball of the night;

Tiger burning cream and red
and black accompanies
an Elephant in pink –
fresh from willowherb
and woodbine lick;

Convolvulus cavorts
with carmine Cinnabar,
proboscis sucking sweet
from bindweed's
counter-clockwise creep;

Next comes ghostly Vapourer
with rare Blue Underwing,
drifting on the scent of thyme
then resting side by side
on lichen-covered rock;

Joining them in beam
of bright: Lackey, Eggar,

Moth Ball

Magpie, Footman, Fox
and Goat – until the air
is all a mist of wings,
kaleidoscope afloat;

So let us set it all to music
– Moonlight Serenade
for insect *son et lumière*,
but soon the butterflies
will come as lunar lightness
fades to morning sun;

First Peacock flirts
with Tortoiseshell,
then Red Admirals choose
flowers of buddleia,
scorning Cabbage White
who partners dodge of shadow,
unaware she's all alone.

HOPE HIBERNAL

Rather
I would write
my tale
on running
water
than tell
it you
who are
so loath
to listen
– better
that you
hibernate
in my January
thoughts until
we re-assess
this mess
in the waking
clash
of spring
when I find
you still
on the meniscus
of my mind

Moth Ball

SUMMER HOLIDAY

In childhood journey back
to Wales where I was born,
I remember seeing
a soldier, all alone,
guarding roadside
ammunition dump,
half-covered
by tarpaulin flap.

And barrage balloons
tugging at white hawsers,
connecting them to towns
of Biggleswade and Baldock
– grounded still
in post-war shortages.

The only coloured cars
were old – like ours,
a thirties Hillman Minx
which Father had to crank
in double-breasted
demob suit he wore.

In the fifties then,
ration books still meant
sweetless, meatless

Hear the Colour

times for us –
Mum in triple-knotted
scarf and shoes
so sensible and we brothers
knitted up the same
in stripey pullovers
that turned us into twins.

The Three Pots pub
at Atherstone
was our halfway stop
and we two 'gansie' boys,
trapped in petrol-smelling
back, could get out then
and walk the panting dog.

Earlier, in Colchester,
we'd watched our father
pack the car; three things
each, he'd told us,
my choice a ball and fishing
rod and cricket bat.

Later on my brother was to drop
his stamp collection
from the speeding car
– well, forty miles an hour –
and see the road behind
strewn with Egypt's pyramids
and heads of US presidents.

Moth Ball

But Father wouldn't stop
and my brother couldn't speak
for tears – 'til Mother
touched him gently
with a shilling in her hand.

Then, at Gobowen, crossing
border into Wales, we whooped
and cried and marvelled
at the mountains once again
– and headed to the nearest
lake to fill the steaming 'rad'
for that final homeward run:
Porthmadog here we come,
back to where our lives began.

Hear the Colour

MISTER POLLINGTON

You came trotting
down our road
on Friday sunshine days
– you, your two-horse
cart, loaded up
with fruit and veg;

Long shiny hair
you had – we saw it
sticking out
from your wide-brim hat –
and waxed moustache
twirled to pen-nib points;

All dressed in black
you were, with smart
waistcoat buttoned up,
and you waved
a whip to urge
the ageing horses on;

Your wife sat
by your side
and never spoke,
but puffed
on a cheroot
you lit for her;

Moth Ball

Spuds and cabbages
my mother bought,
and you gave her
change from
a leather bus
conductor's bag;

Mister Pollington,
you were a right
dandy of a man
and winked at us
when we stroked
the horses' heads,
and clicked your
tongue and cracked
the whip –
and you were gone.

SWEET 'GALE

Last night I swear
I heard a nightingale
– grace notes rising
to crescendo gurgling,
a heart and soul
on journey way beyond
our earthly register.

From where it sang
the misty dewdrop air
weighed wet with scent
of myrtle bog – sweet
gale by other name;
a sound and smell
that blent so well
in mystic summertime.

Moth Ball

TIME CUTTER

Sweet sweeps of grass
laid low;
red prick of poppy,
that universal sigh;
relentless twist
and curl
as he lets his arms unfurl
– a swishing pendulum
restoring contours to the ground,
scythed in layered lines
of lushiness,
yellowed now by mourning sun;
the Time Cutter's job
is done –
but life goes on.

Hear the Colour

CRITH OF A HERON

In that warm follicle of a moment,
bent in stillness of her essence, she waits
– for ever if she must – to pounce;
zig-zagged in that awful ticking roundelay,
standing ready to detect every
little movement within her chosen
stream of consciousness – integral unzipped,
yet zipped upon itself; argal to act,
she rehearses inwardly, as turmoil
licks the arching tuck. It is the crith.

Chance will only come the once – take it;
entriggered by her mounting hunger,
she cannot miss that moment of release;
to be, to act – to act, to be, there is
no other way for bankside heron
to pass the day: assume that striking pose,
seize the moment – Prometheus unbound
yet bound to re-begin, endlessly;
when the moment's here, beak is but a spear
and finning fish have everything to fear.

All this I know as I was there, watching
too – unseen, unbeknownst to stock-still bird;
for two hours plus we were bound together
by the rushy rhythm of our river;

Moth Ball

such steady concentration made me one
with flowing water – to act, to be,
to be, to act – until, eventually,
I barely saw the flash, the straightened zed
of neck, as spotted trout was deftly spiked
and carried off in clumsy climbing flight.

Hear the Colour

SILVER ADDER

Coiled fatly on a rock,
the adder sucked in strength
from the body-heating sun
and made ready for the hunt.

Its squat, arrow head
hid folding fangs,
ready primed with searing
yellow sting – enough
to stop a rabbit dead.

The only movement came
from its deeply-forked
black tongue as it
licked the scent of prey
from off the mountain air.

Along its stubby length
a dark zig-zag
announced its
viperous identity.

Meanwhile, a buzzard circled overhead ...

The snake, a silver
mutant, not the usual
bracken-brown, melded

Moth Ball

in so well with its
grey bog habitat.

And on the other side of the rock ...

A young boy sat near,
unaware,
as he listened
for the noise that brought
him to the heather
hummock by the rock.

Soon it came, a distant hum
that rent the sky,
increasing in intensity
as vibrations shook
the dry cracked earth.

The adder couldn't hear
the deafening drone,
but felt the thrumming sound;
slowly, it lifted its brutal
head, swaying side to side
as its tongue tasted air.

Coiled tightly now,
it sensed the smell
of prey; but still
its coral-black eyes
could not find the target,
hidden by a tussock hump.

Hear the Colour

The boy looked up
and saw the aeroplane
– Flying Fortress, four
engines (reciting to himself),
B-17, crew of ten,
nine-bomb capacity.

Behind the bomber came
seven more, but that
was all (four missing,
thought the boy) .

His sadness grew
as the planes flew on;
and then he saw
a fluttering sheen of silver
as tiny strips of radar-fooling
screen cascaded down to him.

One fell upon the adder's
rock and the boy
reached out in search of it.

His cry of pain
was drowned
by the sound
of the last returning plane.

And as the striking adder
crawled away,
the circling buzzard
swooped on the spent, fat snake

Moth Ball

and soared aloft
with its poisoner prey.

The boy, trying not to cry,
staggered down the hill,
clutching his swelling
hand which still held
the silver from the sky.

BOYHOOD MAN

Put away childish
things; now's the time
to know reality –
that fairy tales
were just a load of tat,
told to slake
the young imaginings.

And yet, and yet
I hesitate to let go
altogether, for the boy
within the man
– the cave behind
the waterfall –
is for ever beckoning.

These yearnings then
are the music
of the mind, playing
continuously – until
the profoundest
sequence of the anthem
is finally resolved.

Moth Ball

WORDS IN STONE

You, who fashion grace from bronze and stone
– and I who stone my memories with ink,
can we ever make that link beyond
a glance or flickered look across a flame?
I pile up questions in my mind, never
to be put lest you turn to chisel shapes
from rough of your own marbled thoughts
– seeing only unformed musings out of reach;
thus we walk, in opposite direction,
and pass without a single backward look:
you to sculpt and I to mess with words.

Hear the Colour

RED

Red is the nipple
of your heart,
the blush I feel
for you
when I am wrong
and you
are right,
a colour you don't
see until
the light
comes streaming
in the window
once again.

www.ingramcontent.com/pod-product-compliance
Lightning Source LLC
Chambersburg PA
CBHW022119040426
42450CB00006B/763